P9-DCC-251

ANCHORAGE

LIFE AT THE EDGE OF THE FRONTIER

CLARK JAMES MISHLER

YesAlaskaPress
ANCHORAGE ALASKA

Perched at the edge of the Alaskan wilderness, the Anchorage skyline glistens in the early evening light as viewed from the Tony Knowles Coastal Trail near Pt. Woronzof.

nchorage's office buildings and hotels shine in the early evening light in this southwest bird's-eye view of downtown's central core.

Coca-Cola

Life at the Edge of the Frontier

by Clark James Mishler

Some months ago, while attempting to explain my soon to be published photo book about Anchorage, I told my old friend, Nancy Gordon: "I would be happy with either of two reactions from locals to the book; 'He got it!' or, 'Gee, I didn't realize what a great place Anchorage is!' " Nancy paused for a moment and said "I get it; this will be the book we can send to our friends and relatives back east to prove we didn't make a mistake by coming here 35 years ago!" Nancy was, of course, right on; it is entirely abut us and our never ending need to promote Anchorage and, for that matter, Alaska to our friends, relatives and just about everyone we meet anywhere in the world.

I love living in Anchorage; a city large enough to have more activities than any one human could attend, while retaining some of those qualities that one usually associates with small communities. As an example, some months ago I was walking to my car in downtown when, suddenly, a truck came to a screeching halt. As the window rolled down, I could see the driver, a business associate with a sense of urgency on her face. "Clark," she yelled through the open window, "a half a block back ... there's a stuffed caribou in the back of a pickup!" Then, just as suddenly, the window powered up and off she sped. Reversing course, I headed in the direction she had indicated and, sure enough, the resulting image was exactly my kind of photograph-provocative and humorous.

Whether it's a friend telephoning me about a moose on the Anchorage Park Strip with a string of Christmas lights in his antlers or a beautiful flower garden in a remote east Anchorage neighborhood, my many Anchorage friends are always watching out for me; they are my extra sets of eyes.

Anchorage is not the perfect city but it is safe to say that it is a much better city today than it was when I arrived over 35 years ago. In that time, Anchorage has grown to twice its size. With that growth have come some of the problems that plague most American cities of 278,000 people. Overcrowded schools, crime and, yes, even traffic jams are all a part of Anchorage's fabric as we try to keep pace with continuing growth and expansion. This book is not about Anchorage's problems nor does it attempt to illustrate things about Anchorage that are less than positive. This book, for all practical purposes, features some of those things we love about Alaska's largest city. To a certain extent, it is about the architecture, mountains, vistas, wildlife and flowers. Mostly, though, its about the people who live here, those crazy individuals who, for what ever reason, have decided to make Anchorage their home. They come from all over America, all corners of the world and even from the tiny villages throughout Alaska. Together, we have come to this place and formed a wonderful community with unlimited opportunities and boundless energy!

It has been said that Anchorage is not Alaska but you can see it from here. Anchorage may not be everyone's ideal Alaska but it is an exciting city in a beautiful setting, inhabited by some of the most diverse and gracious people anywhere. It is my hope that the images contained here will offer a glimpse into this wild and wonderful place we call home ...our life at the edge of the frontier.

Anchorage Moose (left), with their massive antlers, are infamous for stripping trees of their leaves and, occasionally, strings of electric lights. A mounted caribou head (above) protrudes from the back of a pickup in downtown Anchorage.

Money flows with music, dancing, and fundraising for the victims of Hurricane Katrina. Over 800 Alaskans signed on with the American Red Cross of Alaska as disaster response volunteers and 200 were deployed to the Gulf states to provide desperately needed help and hope.

Fur hats, parkas and warm smiles are worn by Eagle River resident Russ Wilmot, who volunteers each year at the ceremonial start of the Iditarod in downtown Anchorage. Over 1,800 volunteers assist the Iditarod effort in Anchorage and throughout the state.

The Mount Edgecumbe Yup'ik Dancers (right) perform at the Alaska Federation of Natives Convention. AFN, held each October, is a great opportunity for Alaska's Native people from all regions of Alaska to meet, discuss issues, and set policy. Highlights of the event include traditional Native dancing exhibitions and the AFN Crafts Fair.

Fire on Ice, the annual New Year's Eve celebration hosted by the Anchorage Downtown Partnership and the IBEW, is a popular family event. This combination photograph features the skating party at Town Square which is immediately followed by a spectacular year-ending fireworks display.

Hilton

The container ship, m/v Horizon Kodiak, departs the Port of Anchorage at 11:30 PM and heads south past Mount Susitna during Anchorage's long summer twilight. Along with Totem Ocean Trailer Express, these ships bring 80% of all goods consumed by 80% of Alaskans through the Port of Anchorage.

Garden tour participant, Krista Shelby, pauses to enjoy the carefully appointed garden designed by Camille Williams in her east Anchorage neighborhood. Anchorage's intense summers and rich soil make gardening a natural lifestyle choice for many members of the community.

anding a small plane at Anchorage's Merrill Field at sunset reminds you of the important connection between the single engine bush plane and the thousands of square miles of wilderness just a few minute's flight from Anchorage.

You need not charter a plane and fly to a remote Alaskan lodge to land that trophy salmon. Instead, head down to Anchorage's Ship Creek, rent a rod and reel, purchase some bait, and try your hand at landing the big one just a few minutes' walk from the center of downtown.

Each October trumpeter swans migrate to Potter Marsh and other wetlands along the Seward Highway, where they fill up on roots prior to their long migration to warmer climates. Bring your bicycle and enjoy the crisp fall evenings along the new trails paralleling the

Originally reserved as a landing strip for Anchorage's first biplanes, the Park Strip is now a gathering place for festivals and community celebrations. The annual Fourth of July parade culminates at the Park Strip (right) where the Anchorage Fire Department offers a bird's-eye view of the revelers. The annual Oceans Festival (above) celebrates Alaska's oceans, coast line, and sea life with music, food and water activities.

UNOCAL
FIRE
Class 1
FLOWMINDER
SMART
GALLONS PER MINUTE
LOWER
RAISE
RIGHT
LEFT
EXTEND
RETRACT
Class 1

ANCHORAGE FIRE STATION 14
4501
ANCHORAGE
14
OL NAVY

Captain James Dennis and his crew welcome young visitors from "Camp Healthy Kids" during a field trip to Anchorage Fire Station 14 in east Anchorage.

Senior Airman Elizabeth Delaney (left) performs with the US Air Force Band of the Pacific in the Anchorage Fourth of July Parade. Anchorage's Fort Richardson and Elemendorf Air Force Base experienced considerable growth during and after World War II and have contributed greatly to the economy and population of Alaska's largest city.

The Fourth of July parade offers Anchorage's diverse ethnic communities an opportunity to strut their stuff. Exotic floats, costumes, and musical instruments illustrate the cultural pluralism that defines Anchorage's population. It is, therefore, no surprise that the Fourth of July is one of Anchorage's most popular community events.

With more Native Alaskans than any other community in Alaska, Anchorage has earned the title as the state's "biggest village." Families from all regions of Alaska have been drawn to Alaska's most diverse community and have brought with them a wide variety of cultures and languages. Inupiaq from northern Alaska, Yup'ik and Cup'ik from southwest Alaska, Athabaskans from interior Alaska, Aleut and Alutiiq from Alaska's Aleution Chain and Eyak, Tlingit, Haida and Tsimshian from southeast Alaska have, for various reasons, made their homes in Anchorage.

When Gladys Johnson (left) moved to Anchorage from Hooper Bay in 1983, she brought her culture, her colorful kuspuks, and a love for "Native food." Each fall, Gladys spends many days in Anchorage's Arctic Valley filling her bucket (and her freezer) with the annual bounty of blueberries and blackberries. At her suburban home in South Anchorage (right), Gladys treats her visiting kids and grandchildren to a traditional meal of dried white fish, walrus, caribou, goose soup, dried salmon, fresh greens with herring eggs and agutak, a mixture of fat, white fish, salmonberries, blackberries, and blueberries.

Moose sightings within the Anchorage basin are always a treat and, luckily, a regular occurrence. While generally docile, keep your distance as these giant ungulates like their space.

Those who live in one of the high western-facing Anchorage neighborhoods (collectively known as the "Hillside") enjoy a great view of Anchorage, Turnagain Arm, and the sun setting behind the Alaska Range.

Coming face to face with a bear might be a frightening experience unless, of course, his name is Jake. This ten-foot, six-inch, 1,400 pound Kodiak Brown Bear has lived at the Alaska Zoo in Anchorage since being orphaned over 20 years ago. A perennial favorite with visitors, Jake is one fun-loving and playful bruin.

Spotting a caribou on the streets of Anchorage may not be as unusual as one might think. During the summer months, Star and her care-taker, Albert Whitehead and his grandchildren, Amanda and Jenna Seaman, can be spotted walking Star through Anchorage's downtown neighborhoods.

Giro
Giro
BELL
sport

Young women (left) approach the starting line for the new sport of roller-skiing at Anchorage's Kincaid Park while a competitor (above) sprints toward the finish line.

A cosmopolitan campus in a stunning setting, the University of Alaska Anchorage, with the new UAA/APU Consortium Library (right), is a public square for Alaska's largest city and a laboratory of ideas for some 20,000 students. UAA's Dr. Brian Wick, Professor of Mathematics (left), is the recipient of the Chauvenet Prize for his work in Gaussian Primes theory. The UAA Debate Team (below) has long been among the best in the country. Their recent tie for fifth place among 336 teams competing in the 2007 World Universities Debating Championships, proves the Seawolf team of Tom Lassen and Chris Kolerok to be among the best in the world.

Heading south past Potter Marsh, the Seward Highway is the single road for access to the communities along Turnagain Arm, Turnagain Pass, and the popular Kenai Peninsula.

What is the future of Anchorage? Does anybody know?

by Michael Carey

Professional forecasters seem to come from two schools. First are the gradualists who believe tomorrow will be similar to today - the assumption most of us make about our own lives. Change to them is modest evolution, proceeding slowly. Standing in sharp contrast are the visionaries, the prognosticators of radical change. Often enough, these visionaries cite astonishing new technology, rapid population shifts, or exceptional natural forces - as in global warming. If the visionaries get really fired up, they insist we soon will be living on the moon, driving cars fueled by hemp or fleeing coastal lowlands as the polar ice caps melt.

When Anchorage was founded in 1915, Alaska visionaries - usually newspapermen who had been listening to a politician - could see a grand future built on the territory's "vast storehouse of natural resources." They foresaw millions of cans of salmon, tons of coal, immeasurable board-feet of timber, and deposits of gold, silver and other minerals that, when developed, would make Alaskans as rich as Rockefeller. "Fairbanks," one pundit said, "would become the next Kansas City." Little was said about oil.

Anchorage economist Neal Fried says, "It is just as likely that some radical event will shape the future as it is tomorrow will be similar to today." World War II was a "radical event," and after statehood, Anchorage experienced two "radical events," both unanticipated and unpredicted: the March 1964 earthquake and the Prudhoe Bay oil-lease sale of 1969. The quake rearranged the face of downtown Anchorage and had the curious effect of providing Anchorage with unimaginable free publicity, as many Americans who had never heard of the city learned of it through the disaster. Oil development reshaped the community's face, too, as Anchorage became the corporate headquarters for the oil industry in Alaska. It may seem shocking to a 21st-century mind, but a youngster growing up in Anchorage - or Fairbanks - in the late '50s or early '60s could graduate from high school without meeting anyone in the oil industry. That would be unlikely, if not impossible, today.

At 90 years of age, Anchorage is a city of 278,000 people. About four in ten Alaskans live here. Anchorage is in every sense a modern city. The gap between Anchorage and "the states" - in communications, income, cost of living, even fashion - is modest. The latest trends may not reach Anchorage as quickly as they engulf lower Manhattan or San Francisco, but they do arrive far more rapidly than 50 years ago when they seemed to travel slow freight.

If we accept the gradualists' approach to forecasting Anchorage's future, what do we see? Anchorage has become a magnet for minority and immigrant populations as families from all over the world have been drawn to Alaska for economic opportunity. As Julia O'Malley reported in an outstanding series in the *Anchorage Daily News*, minorities now comprise 30 percent of the Anchorage population; nearly half the local school children are members of minority groups. Who would have predicted this at statehood? Probably nobody.

The growing minority presence, especially minorities with an international background, is reflected in all facets of Anchorage life, from business, especially restaurants, to the court system (where interpreters are often required for new Alaskans who don't speak English). If you want to experience the new diversity first hand, Julia O'Malley suggests you watch fellow shoppers in the big box stores, but you can see the same thing riding the People Mover bus system. Indeed, all over North America public transportation has become home to the United Nations with passengers in traditional garb speaking many languages into their cell phones.

If tomorrow is like today, then we will see more Pacific Islanders, more Koreans, more Filipinos, more Hispanics - and yes, more Alaska Natives who either grow up here or choose Anchorage over rural Alaska because of the city's

As viewed from Point MacKenzie, Anchorage glows in the evening sun as a passenger jet turns south over Cook Inlet (left). Sophia Chya and Serenity Schmidt (above), with traditional Alutiiq headdresses and face tattoos, from the Alaska Native Heritage Center.

economic opportunity. It's logical that there also will come a time that these immigrants, building on their success, will enjoy far more economic and political power than they do today. To an occasional Anchorageite change can be disturbing - for example, the gentleman who called the *Anchorage Daily News* editorial staff to complain that Anchorage is becoming "too much like San Francisco." When informed that this might not be bad, the man expressed a longing for the "real Anchorage," the community he encountered when he drove the Alaska Highway in the '50s.

If tomorrow is like today, Anchorage also will become older, according to state and municipal figures. By 2018, the state projects, one in eight residents of Anchorage will be 65 years of age or more, close to double the percentage today. As recently as 1980, only one in fifty residents was 65 or older. If, as the Alaska Department of Labor suggests, more than 36,000 seniors are living in Anchorage in 2018, they will form an important and interesting voting block - far more concerned about affordable medical care and prescription drugs than snow machine trails and skateboard parks. Presumably, those who do not continue working also will have more free time to devote to civic activities.

Finally, if tomorrow if like today, we will see more emphasis on civic betterment and beautification from people of all ages. Anchorage has had a strong commitment to both since at least the '50s, when both were harnessed to the statehood movement, but betterment and beautification have always been in conflict with Alaska's libertarian streak - the "I-don't-give-a-damn-how-they-do-it-Outside" mantra. That mantra will continue to have an audience, but the audience, at least in Anchorage, is in decline. People don't just want roads, they want roadside amenities that please the eye.

If Anchorage succumbs to economist Fried's "radical event," what form would the event take? If any of us live long enough, global warming might be the answer. You don't have to imagine palm trees along Cook Inlet to understand that a change of a few degrees year-around could not only change the daily weather and overall climate but influence how people feel about the weather. Winter cold is, after all, one of Alaska's defining characteristics - and a source of Alaskans' complaints.

Anchorage's economy can expect ups and downs - perhaps even recessions like that of the mid-'80s - but radical lasting change would probably be the result of changes in the nation's economy or changes in national policy toward Alaska. For example, if Americans use far less oil - if substitutes become common - the effects would be felt all across Alaska and could be dramatic. The decline of the Prudhoe Bay oil field and the failure of the oil companies to find and develop new fields could produce similar consequences. Changes in federal policy that might influence Anchorage would include a decline in federal spending or a new military doctrine that de-emphasizes Alaska.

After the 2006 election, a university professor told *USA TODAY*, "We've become less isolated, more cosmopolitan, less the Last Frontier..." The professor teaches at the University of New Mexico; he was describing changes in his state and throughout the mountain west. But he could have been talking about Anchorage. We are indeed far less isolated than in the past, far more cosmopolitan, and if we continue to pay homage to Last Frontier traditions, we are well aware that Anchorage 2006 is not Nome 1906 - or Anchorage 1956. We enjoy watching fishermen battle salmon in Fish Creek, but we are more apt to enjoy eating salmon prepared by a chef in a first-class restaurant.

We also enjoy watching moose browse casually in the front yard or ambling indifferently through heavy mid-town traffic. Indeed, the moose with a set of Christmas lights adorning his rack has become a stock Anchorage character, his image sent around the world via the Internet; he's the cosmopolitan moose.

As we look to the future, we can see that whether change is gradual or radical, Anchorage will remain with a special blessing: a jewel of a setting. Few cities have the ocean at their front door and a serious mountain range at their back. Few cities have as much public land open to recreation within their boundaries. Fewer still have such rapid access to boundless wilderness.

If you live in Anchorage long enough, you begin to take the city for granted. That's why it can be such a pleasure to talk to newcomers just discovering the community. Maybe they're a bit apprehensive finding themselves so far from family and friends - whether family and friends are in Manila, San Jose or the remote village of Shaktoolik - but they also are so excited by Anchorage's natural beauty and opportunities, they will tell you, "Anchorage has so much to offer. I'm not leaving." And, in the end, we are the happy beneficiaries of this influx of cultures. We are richer in so many ways that, we too, are not leaving any time soon.

—Michael Carey is the former editorial page editor of the Anchorage Daily News, a freelance writer and television host of KAKM's Anchorage Edition.

The annual Fourth of July parade (above) features members of Anchorage's diverse cultures, including the Karilagan Folkloric Group of the Filipino Community. Dogs and master (right) exercise during an evening walk on the Tony Knowles Coastal Trail.

Twenty foot red steel points, a detail of *Crystal Lattice* by sculptor Robert Pfitzenmeier, stand near the entrance to the Anchorage Museum of History and Art.

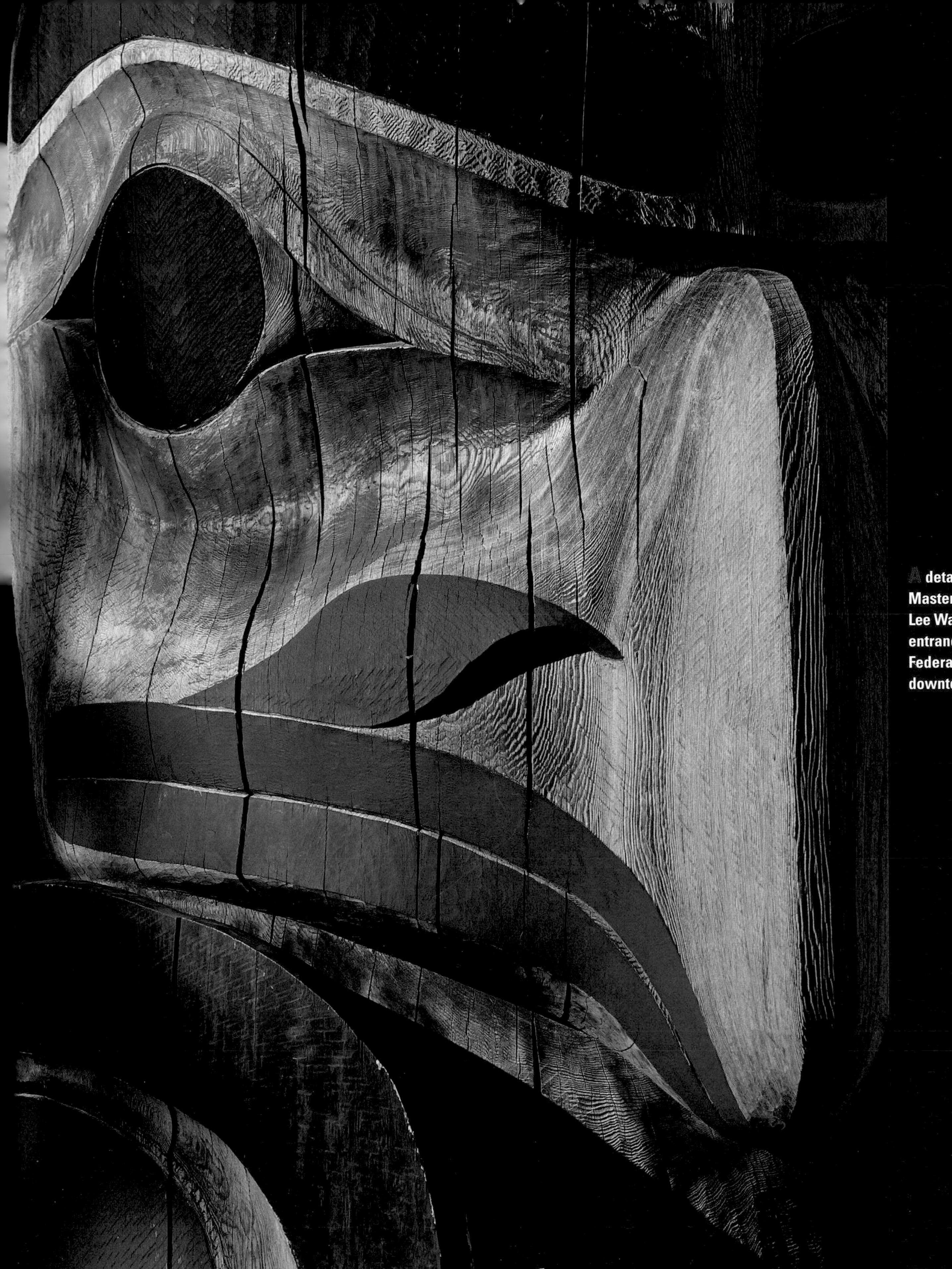

A detail of a totem by Master Tlingit Carver Lee Wallace protects the entrance of the Nesbett Federal Court House in downtown Anchorage.

NORDSTROM

Anchorage's Fifth Avenue Mall (left) features the national chain stores, local boutiques, and Alaska collectables. Elsie Graham (above) will help you find the perfect gift in the Nordstrom Men's Department.

LEFT LANE
ONLY
ONLY
ONE WAY
TURNING TRAFFIC MUST

Twilight features a backdrop of Cook Inlet and the Alaska Range while man-made lights begin to illuminate the downtown Anchorage streets.

BUCS RADIO
MILNER
20

Long before they made it to the "Bigs," many major league baseball players, including Mark McGuire, Dave Winfield, and Barry Bonds, got their start as college all-stars playing in the Alaska Baseball League. Mulcahy Stadium, home to the Anchorage Glacier Pilots and the Anchorage Bucs, is the perfect venue for a great game of baseball during Anchorage's glorious summers. Golfers, too, have many opportunities to enjoy Anchorage's summer with four 18-hole courses, complete with foxes, wolves, moose, eagles, and the opportunity to play until midnight.

Inupiaq and Athabaskan artist and board member for the Alaska Native Arts Foundation, Sonya Kelliher-Combs, presents her creation titled *Secrets,* produced from traditional materials including seal gut and porcupine quills.

The downtown Anchorage skyline (right) reflects in Cook Inlet as two lovers (above) pause near the Captain Cook Monument at Resolution Point.

Philip Blanchett and John Chase (left) sing and beat traditional Yup'ik drums at a dedication celebration at the Alaska Native Heritage Center. Members of the Alaska Native Heritage Dancers (above) rehearse on stage at the Alaska Center for the Performing Arts in Anchorage.

Home to Olympic medalists, Alyeska Resort is one of the most challenging downhill slopes in the world. Local ski enthusiasts (right) enjoy the view on a warm February afternoon.

BRIKO

two hour drive from Anchorage on the Parks Highway, just north of the Talkeetna Road cutoff, Mount McKinley's south face looms above the treetops.

Sound

One of the most popular day-trips out of Anchorage is a tour of Prince William Sound. This coastal wilderness is just 60 miles from Anchorage and contains more than 3,500 miles of coastline. Shaped by glaciers, earthquakes, rain, and ocean water, this wild Alaskan environment is home to brown bears, otters, eagles, spawning salmon, killer whales, and noisy colonies of nesting marine birds.

A popular destination from Anchorage is the community of Seward. If the drive along the beautiful Seward Highway is the cake, the Alaska Sealife Center is the icing. While there, don't miss Woody the sea lion, a favorite with children and adults alike.

When conditions warrant and the ice is sufficiently thick, Portage Lake can offer an up-close and personal experience with huge chunks of glacier ice. Whether floating or frozen in place, Portage Lake ice and the surrounding mountains are well worth the one hour ride from downtown Anchorage.

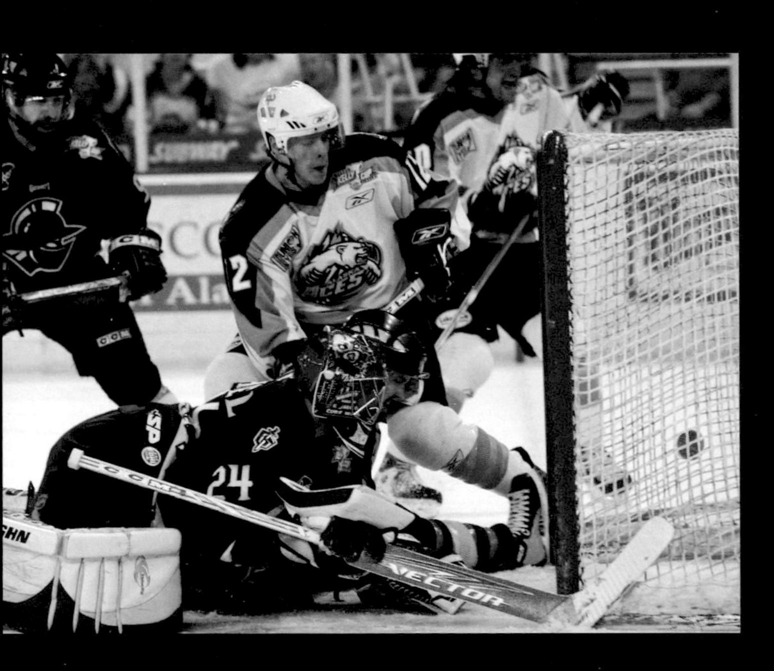

Anchorage's Sullivan Arena is home to some of the best hockey this side of the NHL. The UAA Seawolves hold their own in the very competitive WCHA while the Alaska Aces (above) score a goal on their way to the Kelley Cup Championship. The recipient of the Ace's "Greatest Fan" award, Bobby Hill (right), excites the crowd to the tune of the William Tell Overture.

ACES
ALASKA
FORCE

1401

he Fleischer home (left) in Anchorage's South Addition neighborhood welcomes Christmas guests with paper luminaria. The Mense-Headley home (above) in Bootlegger's Cove, Lima Ferguson at the annual Festival of Lights celebration, and snow covered trees with holiday lights at Alyeska Resort all brighten Anchorage's long winter nights.

Westchester Lagoon becomes a winter wonderland for ce-skaters, particularly when temperatures drop well below freezing and the moisture in the air crystallizes on the trees creating "leaves of ice." The directional sign-post, in front of the Anchorage Log Cabin Visitor nformation Center, sports a rich coat of ice crystals.

Long-time Government Hill resident, Bobbie Bianchi, sits among her flowers outside her historic Cottage #12.

Anchorage business owner, Eleanor Andrews, relaxes in the living room of her condominium near Merrill Field.

Lilly Tuzroyluke demonstrates her athletic talent at a blanket toss demonstration at the Alaska Native Heritage Center in Anchorage.

Photographed at fish camp in Anchorage in 1918, this image of K'enaht'ana (Knik) Dena'ina Athabaskans was part of a series produced by the Alaska Engineering Commission to document the construction of the Alaska Railroad. Many local Dena'ina worked for the Alaska Railroad and aided in its construction. The Dena'ina had fish camps throughout the Anchorage bowl well into the 1950's when expansion of Anchorage resulted in the loss of these traditional camps.

Photo courtesy of UAA Archives & Special Collections, APU Anchorage Historic photographs

Early residents of Anchorage's tent city on Ship Creek (right) gather to bid on land during the auction of 1915.

Photo courtesy of the Anchorage Museum at Rasmuson Center

Anchorage, A History of the "Chosen" Land

by Jack Roderick

When I first arrived in Anchorage to live in 1954, only two city streets - 4th and 5th - were paved. A small town on America's "Last Frontier," Anchorage had about 30,000 residents then, including several thousand military, most of whom lived on Elmendorf Air Base and the Army's Fort Richardson, both on the outskirts of town. In those days, many military lived in the Mountain View neighborhood, then a very active community. Each morning we'd pick up our mail at the downtown post office in the old federal building at the corner of 4th and F, and meet friends. Everyone came to the post office each day to pick up their mail because there was no home mail delivery.

Everything in Anchorage it seemed then, including the U. S. government-owned Alaska Railroad, was run from and controlled by Washington, D.C. We called it "Outside." Still do. "That must mean you live Inside," joked Adlai Stevenson, on a campaign stop during the summer of 1956. Stevenson was running against Dwight Eisenhower for President of the United States. He made his remark while standing on the pitcher's mound in the old baseball diamond at 6th and C. Once the city police station, it now will be the site of the new municipal museum addition. We, seated in the baseball stadium, chuckled of course at Adlai's remark, but I recall at the time thinking that perhaps we were inside something special. Else, why would we want to live in such a cold, wintery place, so far from the rest of America? Perhaps we were crazy. I knew I wasn't crazy, or at least I didn't think so, so it must be that we were somehow different, perhaps even special. I guess I still think that way.

I now tell "Outsiders" that Anchorage is an exciting place to live. Always has been. Something new is always happening. It's like being on an escalator always moving up to a brighter future. We're still helping to build a new community. And then there's the clean, fresh air - year-round.

When on April 9, 1915, President Woodrow Wilson announced that the U.S. government would build a railroad from Seward on the Gulf of Alaska to Fairbanks in Alaska's interior, Anchorage was born. Wilson said the railroad would run through Ship Creek Landing on the shores of Cook Inlet located about midway between Seward and Fairbanks. The rail line would then run north up through the Susitna River valley. Thus, in the summer of 1915, a tent city of some 2,000 entrepreneurs, railroad workers, and camp-followers suddenly sprang up. That summer 600 town lots were auctioned off by the U.S. government bringing in a total of about $150,000.

Also that summer, a Dena'ina boy named Shem Pete came from Susitna Station to Anchorage to try to sell bear skins to the railroad workers and to the six white residents then living along Ship Creek. According to Elizabeth Tower in her book *Anchorage*, U.S. Forester Jack Brown and his wife, Nellie, had their log cabin near the creek's mouth, while another U.S. Forester, Keith McCullough, had his close by. The J.D.Whitneys had their homestead about four miles up the creek, and a squatter named Thomas Jeter had his cabin at the foot of what we now call Government Hill. G. W. Palmer, who around 1900 had a trading post at Knik, across Cook Inlet, now had his warehouse up along the shoreline about three miles north of Ship Creek. (A record of Shem's early entrepreneurial adventures is available in the city's tourist shops.)

But long before President Wilson and Shem Pete did what history books say they did, the Dena'ina (Tanaina) Indians - Shem's ancestors - fished and hunted in what we now call the Anchorage Bowl. Beginning as early as 500 A.D, the Dena'ina had come through the Chugach Mountains from Prince William Sound and from the Copper River Valley to catch salmon in Ship Creek and track rabbits and other animals in the bowl. When in the early 18th century the Russians started gathering furs in the lower inlet they had left the Dena'ina in the upper inlet relatively undisturbed. So, when Captain James Cook sailed up the waters that now bear his name in 1778, he was greeted by friendly Dena'ina in their kayaks. Cook had come north looking for the long-sought-after Northwest Passage, but failing, had turned again to Hawaii, there to be killed by less friendly Indians. And nearly a hundred years after that, in

1867, U. S. Secretary of State William Seward paid the Russians $7.2 million for the 365 million acres that now is Alaska. All this before Anchorage was born.

Soon after the purchase from Russia, white gold prospectors had come through Portage Pass from Prince William Sound into Turnagain Arm. There they made several small discoveries of gold at places like Sunrise City and Hope on the southern shore of the arm. They made a few more at Girdwood on the northern shore. Then, in 1897, gold was discovered at the Klondike in northern Canada. Many miners left Alaska then to seek Klondike gold, but a few remained to look for gold at Nome, Circle City, Rampart, Fairbanks, and other points north. This, again, was all before Anchorage was even a gleam in President Wilson's eye.

Founded as a railroad town in 1915, Anchorage incorporated as a city in 1920. By 1923, the city had grown as far south as 9th Avenue. That summer, Anchorage residents turned out en masse to clear trees from what we now call the Delaney Park Strip. The new air-age had also made pilots like Russ Merrill and Noel Wein anxious to land their small planes at the growing metropolis of Anchorage. So, that summer Frank Reed, later chairman of the Municipal Charter Commission that merged the City of Anchorage and the Greater Anchorage Area Borough into a single Municipality in 1975, carried water to those converting the forest between 9th and 10th into an airstrip.

By 1923, Anchorage's population had grown to about 2,500. By the time legendary newsman Bob Atwood arrived in Anchorage in 1935, the population had grown to about 3,000. "Most Alaskans emigrated at least 2,000 miles to get to their chosen land," wrote Atwood. "Their assets were strong hopes, determined ambition backed up by very little, if any, cash money. But they were young and ambitious in a land with no fences. Less than a half hour away, you can reach snow-capped mountain ranges, many glaciers, fertile salmon streams as well as Native villages, old gold mines and the nation's second largest national forest, where bears, moose and Dall sheep thrive." That's how Bob saw his beloved city. I think it's still true. "We're not ice-bound oddballs," he liked to say.

And about the same time Atwood arrived, 202 Minnesota, Wisconsin, and Michigan families, escaping the Great Depression, were settling on farmland in the Matanuska Valley north of Anchorage. One of the first things done to open Anchorage to the outside world was to build a dirt road all the way from Anchorage up to the Valley. When the first U.S. troops arrived in Anchorage in June of 1940 to occupy the newly-built housing on Fort Richardson and Elmendorf, the June 27 *Anchorage Daily Times* headline blared: "First Troops Arrive." That was a very big day for Anchorage because the presence of the troops would assure the city's merchants continued growth and even survival.

During the next two years, the military constructed the Alcan Highway through Canada, connecting Alaska to the South 48. By then, Anchorage had one paved street - 4th Avenue, and a population pushing 3,500. Then, in 1947, Congress passed Public Law 82, withdrawing 50,000 acres in the Anchorage Bowl for homesteading by World War II veterans. Veterans with names such as Tudor, Boniface, Muldoon, Peterkin, and Kleven filed their claims. By the early 1950s - when I arrived - Anchorage's population - including the military - had grown to slightly over 30,000.

Then, on July 23, 1957, across Turnagain Arm where Captain Cook had turned again, the first commercial oil in Alaska was discovered by Richfield Oil Corporation at Swanson River on the Kenai Peninsula. Eighteen months later, Congress granted us Statehood. When President Eisenhower signed the Statehood Act on Janaury 1, 1959, we became the 49th state, an equal partner with the other "South-48." Again, with an outsized headline, Bob Atwood's *Anchorage Daily Times* blared: "We're In." And we were!

Five years later, a giant earthquake shook us to our muddy roots. And four years after that, in 1968, the two largest discoveries of oil in North America were made at Prudhoe Bay and Kuparuk on Alaska's North Slope. Although Fairbanks lay closer than Anchorage to the new oil fields, Anchorage became the financial and transportation center for the state. It now houses headquarters of several multinational oil companies, seven of the thirteen Regional Native Corporations, and most of the head offices of the major air and marine transportation companies. Within its 1.3 million Anchorage municipal acres are 235 public parks, two universities, four hospitals, a Performing Arts Center, museums, libraries, a large sports center, a Native Heritage Center, and the newly built Convention Center, named for the Dena'ina Indians, the "Original People."

Kay Fanning first arrived in Anchorage from Chicago in 1965. She and her husband, Larry, would buy the *Anchorage Daily News*, and see it become the city's sole surviving daily newspaper. After her arrival in the mid-'60s, Fanning wrote: "Anchorage felt more like the capital of a country than simply the largest city in a sparsely settled state." (I had that same feeling when I had arrived ten years earlier.) To Kay, Alaska felt "more like a new country where people worn from the battles of the 'old country' can find a fresh start and, hopefully, make their fortune as well as enjoy a cleaner environment." Before she moved to Boston in 1983 to become editor of *The Christian Science Monitor* - after having lived here for nearly two decades - Alaska had given her the fresh start she sought.

U.S. Sen. Ted Stevens likes to tell visitors: "If you ever come to Alaska, you will never get all the way home." I believe it, too. "To be an Alaskan," Ted says, "is to share a state of mind." I think he's right again. Think big. Think differently. Where else do people sing the state song before public performances? Where else do they publicly recognize that the land on which they sit once was owned by the Dena'ina - "the First People"? Where else, indeed.

—Jack Roderick, former Anchorage Borough Mayor, and oil historian

Early Anchorage residents turn out in honor of recruits who are about to leave for their training stations, circa 1918.

Photo courtesy of UAA Archives & Special Collections, APU Anchorage Historic photographs

Summer or winter, a horse-drawn carriage is one unique way to enjoy the sights of downtown Anchorage.

Town Square, at the center of the downtown district, features an impressive display of flowers amid quiet spaces.

live and well, the Anchorage arts scene offers something for everyone. Keeping up with all the penings, concerts, and performances can be a study in time management. The monthly First Friday rt Walk (left) challenges art lovers to visit opening night shows at their favorite galleries.

Clockwise) Artist/performer Susan Joy Share with one of her sculptural books. The Anchorage pera features a blend of national and local talent. Artist and arts advocate, Julie Decker, ssembles shows of Alaska content art for the Anchorage Museum of History and Art. Under the irection of Maestro Randall Craig Fleischer, the Anchorage Symphony offers passionate

With her daughter, Rebecca, jazz musician Melissa Bledsoe Fischer encourages competitors with her electric piano at the corner of 15th Avenue and E Street during the Alaska Run for Women. This is one of five major races held each summer that draw runners from around the county to Anchorage's near perfect temperatures, clear air, and occasional moose sightings along the courses.

1860
29
1387
575
529
1745
EAGLES
Baseball

AMARUK
WILDERNESS

Kayaks bask in the evening light at Eklutna Lake, Anchorage's mountain source of fresh water, while a young kayaker learns the basic skills of paddling at the Oceans Festival on the Anchorage Park Strip.

REINDEER

nchorage resident, John Ho (left), enjoys a reindeer sausage sandwich, a local
specialty, served to him by Irene Green on Fourth Avenue in downtown Anchorage
Friends and neighbors (above) meet to enjoy the warm summer sun and delicious
ood at the City Market in Anchorage's South Addition neighborhood

1
Alaska Airlines 2
Alaska Airlines 3
Alaska Airlines
Curb Side Check-in

With a backdrop of Mount Foraker and Mount McKinley, the new C Concourse at the Ted Stevens Anchorage International Airport offers a great first impression for the five million annual travelers who transit the Airport.

Planes are de-iced (above) during a cold morning at Rust's Flying Service on Anchorage's Lake Hood and a turbo Beaver flies over Knik Glacier, just a thirty-minute flight from Anchorage and a favorite destination for local and visiting flightseers.

N754

3009
3009
ALASKA
ALASKA

The Alaska Railroad (left) makes its way toward Anchorage as it parallels the Seward Highway just north of Portage. After a full day of travel south from Fairbanks, visitors (above) alight from Holland America's rail-cars at the Anchorage Railroad Depot.

With an average 81 inches of snowfall each winter and just an hour's drive from Anchorage, Turnagain Pass with its vast open spaces is a favorite destination for snowmobilers and cross country skiers alike.

76

Canadian dog musher, Karen Ramstead (left), drives her team of Siberians down Fourth Avenue during the ceremonial start of the Iditarod on the first Saturday in March while Nichole Fanning and her dog, Ava (above), head to work at a downtown boutique.

Kristine Crossen, of the University of Alaska Anchorage Anthropology Department, examines an ancient mammoth bone collected from a lava tube cave 53 feet below the surface on St. Paul Island in Alaska's Bering Sea.

With the help of Marketing Director Lori Eussen, this telemedicine machine, designed and produced in Anchorage, enables communication with doctors and health care providers in remote villages throughout the state and the world.

ASBN SPORTS
ASBN SPORTS
ALASKA SPORTS BROADCASTING NETWORK
SPORTS 550
Q99.7 Valley Radio
COLONY KNIGHTS

When the last of the leaves have fallen and snow begins to dust the tops of the Chugach mountains, it can't be long before Alaska's top high school teams meet up at the Anchorage Football Stadium. South Anchorage High school hosts Palmer High school in the championship game while South cheerleaders and band member, Mallory Wissing, cheer their team to victory.

Hiking buddies, Marvin Colbert Jr. and Michelle Dickson (left), take a moment to enjoy the view while on their way to the summit of Flattop Mountain, a favorite destination for local hikers. The Zimmer family (above) enjoys an evening walk across alpine tundra near the boundary of Chugach State Park.

In 1971, community activist Lanie Fleischer began a quest to realize her dream of a trail running along Anchorage's mostly inaccessible coastline. Today, the award-winning Tony Knowles Coastal Trail is one of Anchorage's greatest assets. Summer bicyclists, skateboarders, rollerbladers, joggers, walkers, and winter cross country skiers find the ever-changing view irresistible.

Sisters Morelle and Moriah Kinne (left) show off their seedlings at the Anchorage Botanical Garden Fair. This popular annual event is a great opportunity to purchase garden supplies and to simply enjoy the many varieties of carefully nurtured flowering plants.

HANES

University of Alaska Anchorage students take their basketball seriously. As one of eight teams at the Great Alaska Shootout, the UAA Seawolves post up against some of the top Division One basketball teams in the country at this popular pre-season tournament.

As international hubs for Federal Express and United Parcel Service, and with an average of 650 international cargo flight landings a week, Ted Stevens International Airport is one of the busiest cargo airports in the world. Long-time employee Susan Bramstead (right) is the Director of Public Affairs at the Anchorage office of Alaska Airlines.

OPEN
CAUTION
AUTOMATIC
ESCAPE SLIDE
IS ARMED

Downtown Anchorage's Saturday Market is a shopping mecca for visitors and locals alike. The farmers' market in Mountain View is a great place to find fresh fruits and vegetables straight from Alaska's famous Matanuska Valley.

Jill Fredston and Doug Fesler cross country ski near their home in Anchorage's Bear Valley while a cabin defies the cold temperatures of a January evening in Girdwood.

Drive south on the Seward Highway and enjoy one of the top ten "Scenic Byways" in America. Just twenty minutes from downtown Anchorage will reward you with majestic snow-capped mountains, tidal surges, and spectacular 360-degree vistas.

I would like to thank my best friend, Tim Kennedy, who taught me to see and encouraged me to share my photographs. I would also like to thank my friends and associates, Mark Kelley, who has repeatedly encouraged me to produce this book and David Freeman, who has performed his graphic magic to this publication.

Most of all, I want to thank my wife, Mitzi, who has been the ultimate driving force behind this book. Thank you, Mitzi, for your wonderful ideas, your hard work and your never ending love.

Clark James Mishler

Gordon -
Happy Birthday, 2007!
May you continue to enjoy the beauty and bounty of our wonderful city!
Love,
Sue

Yes Alaska Press
1238 G Street
Anchorage, AK 99501

www.YesAlaska.com

First edition 2007

ISBN 0-9652282-7-4

Book Design: David Freeman
Captions Editor: Susan Elliott
Printed in China via Overseas Printing, San Francisco